SHORT TERM DECISION MAKING

Revision Workbook

Teresa Clarke FMAAT

SHORT TERM DECISION MAKING

BY TERESA CLARKE FMAAT

WORKBOOK

Chapter 1 – Introduction

I have written this workbook to assist students who are studying bookkeeping or accountancy. It is not designed as a teaching tool but as a revision workbook. I hope it will help you to consolidate your studies so that you can become more confident with this topic and enable you to feel more comfortable with those tricky exam questions.

We will be working through the following techniques used to aid short term decision making.

- Breakeven point

- Margin of safety

- Target profit

- CS ratio

- Limiting factor calculations

Breakeven point is the volume of sales needed to cover its fixed costs. It is the point at which the business makes no profit or loss. Essentially the point at which the business covers its fixed costs only. This is useful for a business because it shows them the minimum number of units they need to make and sell to avoid making a loss. This is calculated using the formula below.

Note: You will need to remember this. Write down the formulas as you work through this chapter; you will need them in the tasks that follow.

Breakeven point (in units) = <u>Fixed cost</u>
                                 Contribution per unit

Remember: Contribution is sales price less variable costs.

Example:

Rodney makes electric drills and sells them for £100 each. The variable cost per unit is £60. Rodney's total fixed costs are £40,000.

Calculate the breakeven point in units for Rodney.

Breakeven point (in units) = <u>Total fixed cost</u>
                                 Contribution per unit (sales−variable costs)

Breakeven point (in units) = <u>£40,000</u>
                                 £100 - £60

Breakeven point (in units) = <u>£40,000</u>
                                 £40

Breakeven point (in units) = 1,000

<u>Breakeven point = 1,000 units</u>

To calculate this in money or revenue, we multiply the breakeven point in units by the sales price for one unit.

1,000 units x £100 = £100,000

Breakeven point in revenue = £100,000

<u>Margin of safety</u> is the difference in units between the breakeven point and the planned or budgeted sales. The formula for this is below.
Note: You will need to remember this.

Margin of safety (in units) =
budgeted sales in units − breakeven sales in units

<u>Example:</u>

Continuing from the previous example, we know that Rodney had a breakeven point of 1,000 units. If he plans to sell 3,200 units what is his margin of safety?

Margin of safety (in units) =
budgeted sales in units − breakeven sales in units

Margin of safety (in units) = 3,200 − 1,000

Margin of safety (in units) = 2,200

Margin of safety = 2,200 units

Or in revenue:

Margin of safety in revenue (money) multiply the units by the sales price.

Margin of safety in revenue = 2,200 units x £100

Margin of safety in revenue = £220,000

Target profit is the sales volume needed to achieve a certain profit. It is calculated in a similar way to breakeven. The formula for this is below:
Note: You will need to remember this.

Sales volume for target profit = Fixed costs + target profit
                                  Contribution per unit

Example:

Continuing with the example above, Rodney would like to make a profit of £250,000.

Sales volume required to achieve the target profit =

Fixed costs + target profit
    Contribution per unit

Sales volume to achieve target profit =

£40,000 (fixed costs) + £250,000 (target profit)
        Contribution per unit (sales price – variable costs)

Sales volume for target profit = $\dfrac{£40,000 + £250,000}{£40}$

Sales volume for target profit = 7250 units

Or in revenue (multiply by sales price per unit)

7,250 x £100 = £725,000

CS ratio is usually presented as a percentage. This is the contribution to sales ratio as a percentage and can be used to calculate the breakeven point. Exam questions may ask you to calculate this. It is also known as the PV ratio.

The formula for this is:

Contribution per unit / sales price per unit

Exam questions may ask you to give your answer as a percentage in which case you will need to multiply your answer by 100.

We can use the CS ratio to calculate the breakeven point in revenue.

Example:

Using Rodney's figures from above:

Rodney makes electric drills and sells them for £100 each. The variable cost per unit is £60. Rodney's total fixed costs are £40,000.

The sales price is £100 and the contribution is £40.

£40 / £100 = 0.4

To give the answer as a percentage.

0.4 x 100 = 40%

To find the breakeven point using the CS ratio we <u>divide</u> the total fixed costs by the CS ratio.

£40,000 / 0.4 = £100,000

To check this, we divide the revenue by the price per unit of £100 and the answer is 1,000 units, the same answer as we calculated using the breakeven formula above.

<u>Limiting factor</u> analysis is a technique used to firstly identify the limited factor, or scarce resource, needed to produce units and then working through a step-by-step process to rank each product into the order which gives the most contribution per limiting factor, eventually calculating how many of each unit we can produce. For instance, if we want to make two different types of chocolate bar, but have limited chocolate, we will need to decide which one to make first, i.e., the one that is going to make us the most money. Don't worry if this sounds a little confusing, it will become clearer in the examples and tasks.

Example:

Derek was planning to make the following items but has discovered that there is a short of material. He has only 1,000 metres of material.

	Budgeted production	Sales price per item £	Material cost per item £	Material required per item
Shirt	200	50	28	3 metres
Trousers	200	85	56	4 metres

Now we can follow the steps for calculating how many of each item that Derek should produce.

Note: You will need to remember the steps, but they will be much easier when you follow a table (usually provided in your exam).

Step 1: Identify the limiting factor.
This is the material as we were told this in the question.

Step 2: Calculate the contribution per unit for each.

Remember: Contribution = sales price – variable costs

Shirt		Trousers	
Sales price £	50	Sales price £	85
Variable costs £	28	Variable costs £	56
Contribution per unit £	22	Contribution per unit £	29

We can see that the trousers give a higher contribution per unit.

Step 3: Calculate the contribution per limiting factor.

We need to work out which product gives us the best return on the limiting factor.

The shirt requires 3 metres of material.

The trousers require 4 metres of material.

We divide the contribution per unit by the amount of material needed and this will give us the contribution per limiting factor.

Shirt		Trousers	
Sales price £	50	Sales price £	85
Variable costs £	28	Variable costs £	56
Contribution per unit £	22	Contribution per unit £	29
Limiting factor needed	3 metres	Limiting factor needed	4 metres
Contribution per limiting factor £	£7.33 (rounded)	Contribution per limiting factor £	£7.25

Step 4: Rank the products in the order in which they should be made.

The shirts give a higher contribution per limiting factor, so we would make the full budgeted quantity of shirts and use the balance of the material to make as many pairs of trousers as we can.

Step 5: Allocate the limiting factor.

Now we can work out how many pairs of trousers to make and how many shirts to make.

	Budgeted production	Material required per item
Shirt	200	3 metres
Trousers	200	4 metres

200 shirts use 3 metres per shirt.

200 x 3m = 600 metres

We have 1,000 metres of material in total, so this leaves us with 400 metres to make some trousers.

Each pair of trousers requires 4 metres of material.

400 metres / 4 metres = 100 pairs of trousers

We can make 200 shirts and 100 pairs of trousers with the 1,000 metres of material.

Chapter 2 – Tasks with worked answers

Task 1:

Hannah has provided you with the following information about a new product she is planning to make.

Product	Electric cement mixer
Budgeted sales	500 units
Selling price per item	£299
Direct material	£97
Direct labour	£43
Variable overheads	£56
Total fixed overheads	£35,000
Target profit	£25,000

a) Calculate the breakeven point in units.

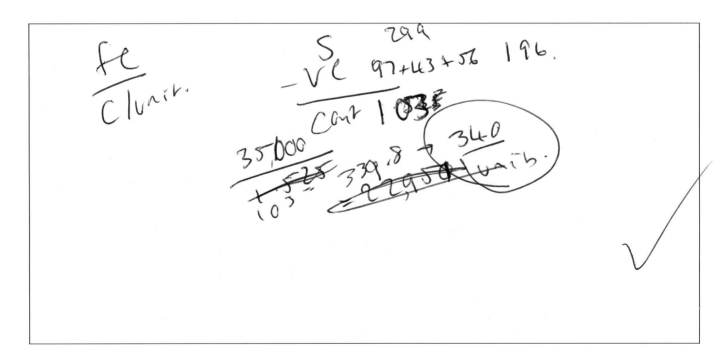

b) Calculate the breakeven point in revenue.

340 units × £299

= £101.660

c) Calculate the margin of safety in units.

500 − 340 = 160 units.

d) Calculate the margin of safety in revenue.

$$160 \times £299$$
$$= £47,840.$$ ✓

e) Calculate the margin of safety as a percentage of budgeted sales.

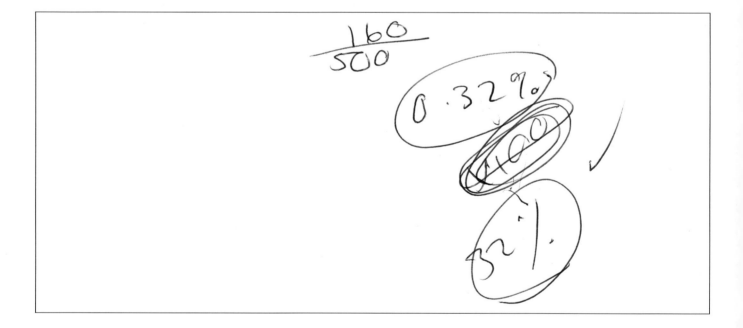

$$\frac{160}{500}$$

0.32% ✓

f) Calculate the sales volume required to achieve the target profit.

$$\frac{FC + TP}{Cont/Unit.} \qquad \frac{35,000 + 25,000}{103}$$

$$S - VC = Cont/Unit. \qquad 583 \; units.$$

Task 1: worked answer

Hannah has provided you with the following information about a new product she is planning to make.

Product	Electric cement mixer
Budgeted sales	500 units
Selling price per item	£299
Direct material	£97
Direct labour	£43
Variable overhead	£56
Total fixed overheads	£35,000
Target profit	£25,000

a) Calculate the breakeven point in units.

Breakeven point = total fixed costs/contribution per unit
(Contribution is sales price less all variable costs)
Breakeven = £35,000/(£299 – (£97+£43+£56))
Breakeven = £35,000/£103
Breakeven = 339.8, so round up because we can't make half a cement mixer!
Breakeven point = 340 units (cement mixers)

b) Calculate the breakeven point in revenue.

Breakeven in revenue is the breakeven point in units multiplied by the sales price per unit.

Breakeven point = 340 units (cement mixers) x £299

Breakeven point in revenue = £101,660

c) Calculate the margin of safety in units.

The margin of safety in units is the difference between the budgeted or planned sales and the breakeven point.

We know that the breakeven in units is 340 units (the answer from a above).

The planned sales are 500 units (taken from the information in the question).

500 units – 340 units = 160 units

The margin of safety is 160 units.

d) Calculate the margin of safety in revenue.

> *The margin of safety is 160 units.*
>
> *To work out the margin of safety in revenue we multiply the margin of safety in units by the sales price of £299 (given in the question).*
>
> *160 units x £299 = £47,840*

e) Calculate the margin of safety as a percentage of budgeted sales.

> *We know that the margin of safety is 160 units (from d above).*
> *We know the budgeted sales are 500 units (from the question).*
>
> *To calculate this as a percentage we take the margin of safety and divide it by the budgeted sales, then multiply by 100 to turn it into a percentage.*
>
> *(160/500) x 100 = 32%*
>
> *Margin of safety as a percentage of budgeted sales is 32%.*

f) Calculate the sales volume required to achieve the target profit.

To calculate the sales volume required to achieve the target profit we use a similar formula to the breakeven formula, but also add in the target profit requirement.

Volume for target profit =

Total fixed costs + target profit/contribution per unit

£35,000 + £25,000 (both taken from information in question)
£103

Volume for target profit = £60,000/£103

Volume for target profit = 582.52

Round up because we can't make half a unit.

Volume of units needed to achieve target profit = 583 units

Task 2:

Robert makes two products, the Kitbar and the Milkykat. You have been provided with the following information about the budgeted sales and costs relating to these products. You have been told that one of the machines has broken down and is waiting to be replaced. This means that only 70,000 machine hours are available.

Product	Kitbar	Milkykat
Budgeted sales	150,000 bars	250,000 bars
Machine hours required for each product	0.2 or 12 minutes	0.25 or 15 minutes
Sales price per unit	£1.90	£2.10
Direct materials per unit	£0.80	£0.70
Direct labour per unit	£0.10	£0.10
Other variable overheads	£0.15	£0.20
Total fixed overheads	£15,000	

a) Complete the table below to calculate the contribution per unit.

Product	Kitbars	Milkykats
Sales price per unit	1.9	2.10
Less variable costs (direct labour, material and variable overheads)	1.05	1.00
Contribution per unit	0.85	1.10
Machine hours required for each unit	0.2	0.25
Contribution per limiting factor (machine hour)	4.25	4.4
Ranking order	2	1

b) Use the table below to calculate how many of each unit Robert should make based on the limiting factor, the limited machine hours available, to maximise the profit.

Product	Kitbar	Milkykat	Totals
Contribution per machine hour (from a above)	4.25	4.4	
Ranking order of products	2	1	
Total machine hours available			70,000
Machine hours allocated to each product	7,500	62,500	
Units made of each product	37,500	250,000	
Total contribution	~~159,375~~ 31,875	~~1,100,000~~ 275,000	~~306,875~~ ~~1,259,325~~
Less fixed costs			15,000
Profit/(Loss)			~~1,244,325~~ 291,875.

Task 2: worked answer

Robert makes two products, the Kitbar and the Milkykat. You have been provided with the following information about the budgeted sales and cost information relating to these products. You have been told that one of the machines has broken down and is waiting to be replaced. This means that only 70,000 machine hours are available.

Product	Kitbar	Milkykat
Budgeted sales	150,000 bars	250,000 bars
Machine hours required for each product	0.2 or 12 minutes	0.25 or 15 minutes
Sales price per unit	£1.90	£2.10
Direct materials per unit	£0.80	£0.70
Direct labour per unit	£0.10	£0.10
Other variable overheads	£0.15	£0.20
Total fixed overheads	£15,000	

a) Complete the table below to calculate the contribution per unit.

Enter the information from the table above into this table. Note that the machine hours per item are less than one hour, but we need to keep it in hours so do this as a percentage. For example, 12 minutes is 0.2 of one hour because 12 minutes / 60 minutes = 0.2.

The contribution per hour is calculated as sales price less all the variable costs.

The contribution per unit is calculated by multiplying the contribution per unit by the hours (or percentage of an hour) that it takes to produce one unit.

Product	Kitbars	Milkykats
Sales price per unit	£1.90	£2.10
Less variable costs (direct labour, material and variable overheads)	£1.05	£1.00
Contribution per unit	£0.85	£1.10
Machine hours required for each unit	0.2	0.25
Contribution per limiting factor (machine hour)	£4.25	£4.40
Ranking order	2	1

The products are ranked according to their contribution per limiting, which is basically their profit per limiting factor.

b) Use the table below to calculate how many of each unit Robert should make based on the limiting factor, the limited machine hours available, to maximise the profit.

Use the information above and the answers you worked out in part a to complete this table.

The contribution per hour and ranking order is entered as per your answers in part a.

The total machine hours available is the limiting factor and this number was given in the question. Enter this as the total machine hours available.

We need to work out how many of each product we can make.

We want to make as many of the Milkykat as possible as this has the higher contribution per limiting factor. The budgeted sales for the Milkykat are 250,000, so we need to calculate how many hours are needed to make that many units.

250,000 units x machine hours required by per unit.

250,000 x 0.25 hours = 62,500 hours. We enter this as the machine hours allocated to the manufacture of the Milkykats.

We work out how many machine hours will be left to make some Kitbars.

Total machine hours available less those allocated to the Milkykat.

70,000 − 62,500 = 7,500 hours

We enter this in the machine hours allocated to the Kitbar.

We know that we can make 250,000 Milkykat bars so we enter this as the unit made of this product.

To calculate how many Kitbars we can make we need to take the machine hours allocated and divide this by the number of hours (or part of hours) that is needed to make one bar.

7,500 / 0.2 = 37,500 units

This is the number of Kitbars that we can make.

The total contribution is calculated by multiplying the contribution per machine hour by the number of machine hours.

Kitbar: £4.25 x 7,500 = £31,875

Milkykat: £4.40 x 62,500 = £275,000

These are entered and then totalled.

The fixed costs, as given in the question are entered into the table.

The profit is calculated by deducted the fixed costs from the total contribution.

Product	Kitbar	Milkykat	Totals
Contribution per machine hour (from a above)	£4.25	£4.40	
Ranking order of products	2	1	
Total machine hours available			70,000
Machine hours allocated to each product	7,500	62,500	
Units made of each product	37,500	250,000	
Total contribution	£31,875	£275,000	£306,875
Less fixed costs			£15,000
Profit/(Loss)			£291,875

Chapter 3 – Tasks

The answers to these tasks are given at the back of the workbook.

Task 3:

Nichols Brooks sell tins of paint. The sales price per can is £8.00. The total variable costs per tin are £3.00. The total fixed costs for the business are £500,000.

a) Calculate the breakeven point in tins.

b) Calculate the breakeven point in revenue.

c) Calculate the amount of tins that Nichols Brooks need to sell to make a target profit of £30,000.

d) The planned sales are 250,000 tins. What is the margin of safety as a percentage of sales?

Task 4:

a) The formula for the breakeven point in units is:

    (i)   Fixed costs / sales price per unit
    (ii)   Fixed costs / contribution per unit
    (iii)   Contribution per unit / fixed costs

b) Contribution is calculated by:

    (i)   Sales price less fixed costs
    (ii)   Sales price less variable costs
    (iii)   Sales price plus variable costs

c) The difference between the breakeven point and the budgeted sales is called the:

    (i)   Target profit
    (ii)   Contribution
    (iii)   Margin of safety

d) The limiting factor is:

    (i)   The resource that is in short supply.
    (ii)   The materials cost of the product.
    (iii)   The number of hours required to make a product.

Task 5:

Archie makes a product called the Viking. The selling price per Viking is £190. The variable cost per Viking is £90. Archie has estimated that the fixed costs for the period will be £30,000.

a) Calculate the budgeted breakeven point in units for the Viking.

b) Calculate the budgeted breakeven point in revenue for the Viking.

c) Archie has asked you to calculate the margin of safety for three different production levels. Use the table below for your answers. Round your answers to the nearest whole percentage.

Budgeted sales in units	500	700	1000
Margin of safety in units			
Margin of safety as a percentage of budgeted sales.			

d) Archie has told you that he would like to make a profit of £12,000 on this process. Calculate how many units he needs to sell to achieve this target profit.

Task 6:

Becky has provided you with the following information.

Budgeted sales volume	35
Budgeted sales price per unit	£6
Budgeted variable cost per unit	£3.50
Total fixed costs	£100
Target profit	£20

Becky has asked you to calculate whether the budgeted sales volume will be enough to achieve her target profit.

Calculate the volume required to achieve the target profit and then draft an email to Becky to advise her of the results.

Calculation:

Email:

To:

From:

Date:

Title:

Task 7:

Carly has provided you with the following information.

Sales price for coffee gift box   £132
Variable costs for the gift box   £44
Total fixed costs   £5,000

a) Calculate the breakeven point in units.

b) If Carly sells 100 gift boxes what is the margin of safety?

c) Calculate the units she needs to sell to achieve a profit of £5,000.

Task 8:

You have been provided with details about two products, the Diamond shower and the Platinum shower.

	Diamond shower	Platinum shower
Sales price	£189	£219
Direct materials	£50	£64
Direct labour	£34	£22
Budgeted sales	200	300

Total fixed costs are estimated to be £50,000.

a) Complete the table below to calculate the total budgeted profit based on the figures above.

	Diamond shower	Platinum shower	Total
Sales income £			
Variable costs £			
Contribution £			
Fixed costs £			
Profit £			

b) Calculate the contribution per unit of each product.

Diamond shower:

Platinum shower:

Task 9:

This task uses the CS ratio to calculate the breakeven point. Exam questions will sometimes ask for this, so take your time with this one.

Teddy sells chairs for £50 each. His variable cost per chair is £40. His fixed costs are £15,000.

a) Calculate the contribution/sales ratio as a percentage.

Note: The contribution/sales ratio is also known as the CS ratio or the PV ratio (profit/volume).

Despite its name, the CS ratio is given as a percentage.

Hint: Use the name of the CS ratio to help you to work this one out.

b) Using your answer to a) above, calculate the breakeven point in revenue.

Note: This method will give you the result in revenue.

c) Check your answer by using the formula to calculate the breakeven point.

Hint: Fixed costs/contribution per unit x sale price

Task 10:

Herringby Products makes a product called the Walker. The selling price of the Walker is £18. The total variable cost per unit is £9.50. The fixed cost for the manufacture of this product is £3,200.

a) Calculate the breakeven point in units for the Walker.

b) Calculate the breakeven point in revenue for the Walker.

c) If Herringby Products makes and sells 500 Walkers, what will be the margin of safety in units?

d) Calculate the margin of safety in revenue.

e) Calculate the margin of safety as a percentage of sales.

f) If Herringby Products wishes to make a profit of £10,000 on this product, how many units will they need to sell?

Task 11:

Teddy Company is planning to make two products this month, the Lumpy and the Yogi. You have been provided with the following details.

	Lumpy £	Yogi £	Totals £
Contribution per unit	750	540	1,290
Fixed costs			80,000
Demand for units	1,000	700	
Labour hours per unit	5	4	

There is a shortage of labour hours this month and only 6,000 hours are available for production of these two products.

Complete the table below to show how many products of each type can be made, along with the forecast profit/(loss) from this process.

Round your answers to the nearest whole pound.

	Lumpy	Yogi	Totals
Contribution per unit £			
Contribution per labour hour £			
Ranking order			
Total labour hours available			
Allocation of labour hours			
Units produced			
Total contribution £			
Less fixed costs £			
Budgeted profit/(loss) £			

Task 12:

a) The large loaf has a selling price of £2.40 and variable costs of £0.60. The fixed costs for this loaf are £100.

Calculate the CS ratio (contribution/sales ratio) as a percentage.

Use the CS ratio to calculate the breakeven point in revenue.

b) The chocolate cake has a selling price of £4.80 and variable costs of £2.40. The fixed costs for this cake are £150.

Calculate the CS ratio (contribution/sales ratio) as a percentage.

Use the CS ratio to calculate the breakeven point in revenue.

c) The vegan pasty has a selling price of £2.50 and variable costs of £0.50. The fixed costs for this pasty are £80.

Calculate the CS ratio (contribution/sales ratio) as a percentage.

Use the CS ratio to calculate the breakeven point in revenue.

Task 13:

Millward Ltd has the provided you with the following information about their new unit, the Shaggy, which they intend to sell for £42 each. They have budgeted for a sales volume of 10,000 units.

		£
Variable costs per unit:	Direct material	7
	Direct labour	5
	Overheads	2
	Total variable costs:	14
Fixed costs per unit:	Overheads per unit	6
Total cost per unit:		20

a) Calculate the total fixed overheads.

b) Calculate the budgeted breakeven point in units.

c) Calculate the margin of safety based on the budgeted sales.

d) If Millward Ltd decide to raise the selling price by £5 per unit what will the impact be on the breakeven point?

The breakeven point will increase.

The breakeven point will decrease.

e) If Millward Ltd decide to raise the selling price by £5 per unit what will the impact be on the margin of safety?

The margin of safety will increase.

The margin of safety will decrease.

Task 14:

a) Describe how to calculate contribution per unit.

b) Write the formula to find the breakeven point in units and explain what breakeven point means.

c) Describe how to find the breakeven point in revenue.

d) Explain how to calculate the margin of safety in units.

e) Write out the formula and explain how to calculate the margin of safety as a percentage of the budgeted sales.

f) Write out the formula to calculate the sales volume required to achieve a target profit and explain what this tells us.

g) Write the formula to calculate the CS ratio (remember to express this as a percentage).

h) Explain what is meant by limiting factor.

Task 15:

You have been provided with the following information about a planned process.

Product	Home working laptop desk
Budgeted sales	1,200 units
Selling price per item	£30
Direct material per unit	£8
Direct labour per unit	£7
Variable overheads per unit	£2
Total fixed overheads	£1,400
Target profit	£15,000

Using the information above, complete the following table.

Contribution per unit	£
Breakeven point in units	
Breakeven point in revenue	£
CS ratio (as a percentage)	
Margin of safety in units	
Margin of safety as percentage of sales	
Sales volume required to achieve target profit	
Total sales income	£
Total variable costs	£
Total fixed costs	£
Budgeted profit	£

Chapter 4 – answers

Task 3:

Nichols Brooks sell tins of paint. The sales price per can is £8.00. The total variable costs per tin are £3.00. The total fixed costs for the business are £500,000.

e) Calculate the breakeven point in tins.

> **Total fixed costs / contribution per unit**
>
> **£500,000 / (£8.00 – £3.00) = 100,000**
>
> **Breakeven point is 100,000 tins.**

f) Calculate the breakeven point in revenue.

> **Breakeven point is 100,000 tins x sale price per tin**
>
> **100,000 x £8.00 = £800,000**
>
> **The breakeven point in revenue is £800,000.**

g) Calculate the amount of tins that Nichols Brooks need to sell to make a target profit of £30,000.

Fixed costs + target profit / contribution per unit

£500,000 + £30,000 / (£8.00 – £3.00) = 106,000

Sales volume to achieve target profit is 160,000 tins.

---

h) The planned sales are 250,000 tins. What is the margin of safety as a percentage of sales?

Difference between the breakeven point and the planned or budgeted sales.
250,000 tins – 100,000 tins = 150,000 tins

The margin of safety is 150,000 tins.

To calculate as a percentage of the sales.

(Margin of safety / planned sales) x 100

(150,000/250,000) x 100 = 60%

The margin of safety as a percentage of sales is 60%.

Task 4:

e) The formula for the breakeven point in units is:

 (iv) Fixed costs / sales price per unit
 (v) **Fixed costs / contribution per unit**
 (vi) Contribution per unit / fixed costs

f) Contribution is calculated by:

 (iv) Sales price less fixed costs
 (v) **Sales price less variable costs**
 (vi) Sales price plus variable costs

g) The difference between the breakeven point and the budgeted sales is called the:

 (iv) Target profit
 (v) Contribution
 (vi) **Margin of safety**

h) The limiting factor is:

 (iv) **The resource that is in short supply.**
 (v) The materials cost of the product.
 (vi) The number of hours required to make a product.

Task 5:

Archie makes a product called the Viking. The selling price per Viking is £190. The variable cost per Viking is £90. Archie has estimated that the fixed costs for the period will be £30,000.

a) Calculate the budgeted breakeven point in units for the Viking.

> **Breakeven point = Fixed costs / contribution**
> **Remember that contribution is sales price less variable costs.**
> **£30,000 / (£190–£90) = 300**
>
> **Breakeven point is 300 units.**

b) Calculate the budgeted breakeven point in revenue for the Viking.

> **To work out breakeven in revenue or money, we multiply the breakeven point by the selling price.**
> **300 units x £190 = £57,000**
>
> **Breakeven point in revenue is £57,000.**

c) Archie has asked you to calculate the margin of safety for three different production levels. Use the table below for your answers. Round your answers to the nearest whole percentage.

Margin of safety is the difference between the breakeven point and the budgeted or planned sales.

Breakeven was calculated above to be 300 units. Deduct this from each of the budgeted sales quantities for the margin of safety.

To calculate the margin of safety as a percentage of sales, divide the margin of safety by the planned sales and multiply by 100.

Budgeted sales in units	500	700	1000
Margin of safety in units	200	400	700
Margin of safety as a percentage of budgeted sales.	40%	57% (rounded)	70%

d) Archie has told you that he would like to make a profit of £12,000 on this process. Calculate how many units he needs to sell to achieve this target profit.

Sales volume to achieve target profit =
fixed costs + target profit / contribution per unit
£30,000 + £12,000 / 100 = 420 units

Sales volume needed to achieve the target profit = 420 units.

Task 6:

Becky has provided you with the following information.

Budgeted sales volume	40
Budgeted sales price per unit	£6
Budgeted variable cost per unit	£3.50
Total fixed costs	£100
Target profit	£20

Becky has asked you to calculate whether the budgeted sales volume will be enough to achieve her target profit.

Calculate the volume required to achieve the target profit and then draft an email to Becky to advise her of the results.

Calculation:

Fixed costs + target profit / contribution per unit

£100 + £20 / £2.50 = 48 units

You could also check the breakeven point in order to advise Becky.

£100 / £2.50 = 40 units

<u>Note</u>: Your email will not be the same as mine, but just make sure you have given her the information she needs.

Email:

To: Becky

From: Teresa

Date: 26 March 2021

Title: Target profit calculations

Good afternoon Becky

I have used your figures to calculate whether your sales volume will be higher enough for you to make your target profit.

Unfortunately, the volume you have budgeted of 40 units is only enough to breakeven. You would need to increase your sales to 48 units to achieve your target profit.

If you need any more information, please let me know.

Kind regards,

Teresa

Task 7:

Carly has provided you with the following information.

Sales price for coffee gift box   £132
Variable costs for the gift box   £44
Total fixed costs   £5,000

a) Calculate the breakeven point in units.

Fixed costs / contribution per unit   **£5,000 / (£132–£44) = 56.81**   **Breakeven point in units is 57 units.**   **Remember we can't make and sell half a giftbox!**

b) If Carly sells 100 gift boxes what is the margin of safety?

Budgeted sales volume – breakeven sales volume   **100 – 57 = 43**   **Margin of safety is 43 units.**

c) Calculate the units she needs to sell to achieve a profit of £5,000.

Fixed costs + target profit / contribution per unit   **£5,000 + £5,000 / £88**   **£10,000 / £88 = 113.63**   **Sales volume to achieve target profit is 114 gift boxes.**

Task 8:

You have been provided with details about two products, the Diamond shower and the Platinum shower.

	Diamond shower	Platinum shower
Sales price	£189	£219
Direct materials	£50	£64
Direct labour	£34	£22
Budgeted sales	200	300

Total fixed costs are estimated to be £50,000.

a) Complete the table below to calculate the total budgeted profit based on the figures above.

The task is asking for the total budgeted profit, so we need to use the sales price and materials costs per unit and multiply by the budgeted sales. All the information is in the table, apart from the fixed costs which are shown below the information table.

	Diamond shower	Platinum shower	Total
Sales income £	37,800	65,700	103,500
Variable costs £	16,800	25,800	42,600
Contribution £	21,000	39,900	60,900
Fixed costs £			50,000
Profit £			10,900

b) Calculate the contribution per unit of each product.

This is asking for the contribution per unit, so you can either go back to the information, which is shown per unit, or use the total in the table above and divide by the sales.

Diamond shower: £21,000 / 200 = £105   **Or from the table:**   £189 − (£54+£34) = £105
Platinum shower: £39,900 / 300 = £133   **Or from the table:**   £219 − (£64+£22) = £133

Task 9:

This task uses the CS ratio to calculate the breakeven point. Exam questions will sometimes ask for this, so take your time with this one.

Teddy sells chairs for £50 each. His variable cost per chair is £40. His fixed costs are £15,000.

a) Calculate the contribution/sales ratio as a percentage.

Note: The contribution/sales ratio is also known as the CS ratio or the PV ratio (profit/volume).

Despite its name, the CS ratio is given as a percentage.

Hint: Use the name of the CS ratio to help you to work this one out.

Contribution to sales ratio is just that.

Contribution/sales as a percentage.

Contribution/sales x 100

(£50–£40)/£50 x 100 = 20%

b) Using your answer to a) above, calculate the breakeven point in revenue.

Note: This method will give you the result in revenue.

> **When using the CS ratio to calculate the breakeven point, we divide the fixed costs by the cv ratio percentage. Yes, that is divide not multiply.**
>
> **Fixed costs / cs ratio**
>
> **£15,000 / 20%**
>
> **£15,000 / 0.2 = £75,000**

c) Check your answer by using the formula to calculate the breakeven point.

Hint: Fixed costs/contribution per unit x sale price

> **£15,000 / £10 x £50 = £75,000**

Task 10:

Herringby Products makes a product called the Walker. The selling price of the Walker is £18. The total variable cost per unit is £9.50. The fixed cost for the manufacture of this product is £3,200.

a) Calculate the breakeven point in units for the Walker.

Breakeven = Total fixed costs / contribution

Breakeven = £3,200 / (£18 – £9.5)

Breakeven = £3,200 / £8.50

Breakeven point in units = 377 (rounded up because we can't make part of a unit)

b) Calculate the breakeven point in revenue for the Walker.

Breakeven in revenue = breakeven point in units x sales price

Breakeven in revenue = 377 units x £18

Breakeven point in revenue = £6,786

c) If Herringby Products makes and sells 500 Walkers, what will be the margin of safety in units?

Margin of safety is the difference between breakeven and budgeted sales.

Budgeted sales 500 units – breakeven units 377 = 123

Margin of safety in units is 123 units.

d) Calculate the margin of safety in revenue.

Margin of safety in revenue is the margin of safety in units multiplied by the selling price of one unit.

123 units x £18 = £2,214

The margin of safety in revenue is £2,214

---

e) Calculate the margin of safety as a percentage of sales.

The margin of safety is 123 units. The budgeted sales figure is 500 units.

Margin of safety/budgeted sales x 100

123/500 x 100 = 24.6%

---

f) If Herringby Products wishes to make a profit of £10,000 on this product, how many units will they need to sell?

Target profit = Total fixed costs + target profit/contribution per unit.

(£3,200 + £10,000)/£8.50 = 1,552.9

Sales volume to achieve required target profit is 1,553 units.

(rounded up as we can't make part of a unit)

Task 11:

Teddy Company is planning to make two products this month, the Lumpy and the Yogi. You have been provided with the following details.

	Lumpy £	Yogi £	Totals £
Contribution per unit	750	540	1,290
Fixed costs			80,000
Demand for units	1,000	700	
Labour hours per unit	5	4	

There is a shortage of labour hours this month and only 6,000 hours are available for production of these two products.

Complete the table below to show how many products of each type can be made, along with the forecast profit/(loss) from this process.

Round your answers to the nearest whole pound.

The contribution per unit is taken from the information table.

The contribution per labour hour is calculated by taking the contribution per unit and dividing by the number of hours it takes to make each product.

The ranking order is the order in which the production should be prioritised to achieve the highest contribution per limiting factor (labour hour).

The total labour hours available was the limiting factor.

Allocate the full amount needed to make the Lump as this was ranked first.

The balance of the hours are allocated to the Yogi.

The units produced is maximum for Lumpy. Yogi units are calculated by taking the labour hours available and dividing by the number of hours required to make one unit.

The total contribution is the units produced multiplied by the contribution per unit OR the labour hours multiplied by the contribution per labour hour.

The contribution from both is added together and the fixed costs deducted. This gives us the forecast profit for the process.

	Lumpy	Yogi	Totals
Contribution per unit £	750	540	1,290
Contribution per labour hour £	150	135	285
Ranking order	1	2	
Total labour hours available			6,000
Allocation of labour hours	5,000	1,000	
Units produced	1,000	250	
Total contribution £	750,000	135,000	885,000
Less fixed costs £			80,000
Budgeted profit/(loss) £			805,000

Task 12:

d) The large loaf has a selling price of £2.40 and variable costs of £0.60. The fixed costs for this loaf are £100.

Calculate the CS ratio (contribution/sales ratio) as a percentage.

Contribution/sales price x 100

(£2.40 – £0.60)/2.40 x 100 = 75%

Use the CS ratio to calculate the breakeven point in revenue.

Fixed costs / CS ratio

£100 / 0.75 = £133.34

e) The chocolate cake has a selling price of £4.80 and variable costs of £2.40. The fixed costs for this cake are £150.

Calculate the CS ratio (contribution/sales ratio) as a percentage.

Contribution/sales price x 100

(£4.80 – £2.40)/£4.80 x 100 = 50%

Use the CS ratio to calculate the breakeven point in revenue.

£150 / 50% = £300

f) The vegan pasty has a selling price of £2.50 and variable costs of £0.50. The fixed costs for this pasty are £80.

Calculate the CS ratio (contribution/sales ratio) as a percentage.

(£2.50 – £0.50) / £2.50 x 100 = 80%

Use the CS ratio to calculate the breakeven point in revenue.

£80 / 80% = £100

Task 13:

Millward Ltd has the provided you with the following information about their new unit, the Shaggy, which they intend to sell for £42 each. They have budgeted for a sales volume of 10,000 units.

		£
Variable costs per unit:	Direct material	7
	Direct labour	5
	Overheads	2
	Total variable costs:	14
Fixed costs per unit:	Overheads per unit	6
Total cost per unit:		20

a) Calculate the total fixed overheads.

We are told that the budgeted sales volume is 10,000 units and the fixed cost per unit is £6.

10,000 x £6 = £60,000

b) Calculate the budgeted breakeven point in units.

> **Fixed costs / contribution per unit**
>
> **£60,000 (from a above) / sales price − variable costs**
>
> **£60,000 / (£42−£14) = 2,142.85**
>
> **Breakeven point is 2,143 units.**

c) Calculate the margin of safety based on the budgeted sales.

> **Budgeted sales are 10,000 units and the breakeven point (from b above) is 2,143 units.**
>
> **10,000 − 2,143 = 7,857 units**

d) If Millward Ltd decide to raise the selling price by £5 per unit what will the impact be on the breakeven point?

If you are unsure about this, try a quick test. The sales price is currently £42 so add £5 to make that £47. Now use that to check the breakeven point.

£60,000 / contribution

£60,000 / (£47 − £14) = 1,818.1, so 1,819 units. This shows us that the breakeven point has decreased with the raised selling price.

The breakeven point will increase.

The breakeven point will decrease.

e) If Millward Ltd decide to raise the selling price by £5 per unit what will the impact be on the margin of safety?

Use the same principle that we did for d above. We can see that with the raised selling price the breakeven point is decreased to so this will give a bigger margin of safety. 10,000 – 1,819 = 8,181. Check back to the previous task and you will see that this has increased.

**The margin of safety will increase.**

The margin of safety will decrease.

Task 14:

Note: Your answers will not be the same as mine! Just make sure that you understand these calculations and can explain them in your own words.

a) Describe how to calculate contribution per unit.

Contribution per unit is the sales price less all the variable costs per unit. The variable costs are all the direct labour, direct materials and variable overheads.

Contribution = sales price – variable costs

Contribution =

sales price – (direct labour, direct materials, variable overheads)

b) Write the formula to find the breakeven point in units and explain what breakeven point means.

Breakeven point in units = fixed costs / contribution per unit

The breakeven point in units gives us the number of units a business needs to produce and sell to cover the fixed costs. It is the point at which there is no profit and no loss.

c) Describe how to find the breakeven point in revenue.

> **To find the breakeven point in revenue, you take the breakeven point in units and multiply it by the sales price of the unit.**

d) Explain how to calculate the margin of safety in units.

> **Margin of safety in units is calculated by taking the budgeted sales and deducting the breakeven sales in units.**
>
> **Margin of safety = budgeted sales – breakeven sales**

e) Write out the formula and explain how to calculate the margin of safety as a percentage of the budgeted sales.

> **Margin of safety as a percentage of sales.**
>
> **Margin of safety / budgeted sales x 100**
>
> **Take the margin of safety and divide this by the budgeted sales, then multiply the answer by 100 to turn it into a percentage.**

f) Write out the formula to calculate the sales volume required to achieve a target profit and explain what this tells us.

Sales volume to achieve target profit =

Fixed costs + target profit / contribution per unit.

The fixed costs and target profit are added together and divided by the contribution per unit.

This calculation tells us how many units the business needs to sell to achieve the profit required, the target profit.

g) Write the formula to calculate the CS ratio (remember to express this as a percentage).

The CS ratio is the contribution to sales ratio.

Contribution / sales price x 100

Take the contribution per unit and divide by the sales price per unit and then multiply by 100 to give the CS ratio.

h) Explain what is meant by limiting factor.

The limiting factor is the scarce resource of process. This could be the hours available or the materials available to make two or more products. If we don't have enough materials to make all the planned products, we need to find out what the limiting factor is and work out the most profitable way to use that resource when planning the production of units.

Task 15:

You have been provided with the following information about a planned process.

Product	Home working laptop desk
Budgeted sales	1,200 units
Selling price per item	£30
Direct material	£8
Direct labour	£7
Variable overheads	£2
Total fixed overheads	£1,400
Target profit	£15,000

Using the information above, complete the following table.

Contribution per unit	**£13 (sales less all variable costs)**
Breakeven point in units	**108 units (fixed costs/contribution per unit)**
Breakeven point in revenue	**£3,240 (108 units x £30)**
CS ratio (as a percentage)	**43.33% (£13 / £30 x 100)**
Margin of safety in units	**1092 units (1,200 – 108 units)**
Margin of safety as percentage of sales	**91% (1092/1200 x 100)**
Sales volume required to achieve target profit	**1,262 units (fixed costs + target profit / contribution per unit)**
Total sales income	**£36,000 (£30 x 1,200 units)**
Total variable costs	**£20,400 (£17 x 1,200 units)**
Total fixed costs	**£1,400 (from table)**
Budgeted profit	**£14,200**

I hope you have found this workbook useful. If you have any comments you can find me on my Facebook page: Teresa Clarke AAT Tutoring.

Teresa Clarke FMAAT

Printed in Great Britain
by Amazon